The Six Miracles
of
Calvary

The Six Miracles
of
Calvary

by

William R. Nicholson

MOODY PRESS
CHICAGO

I challenge the world of Christian literature to produce in the same compass, anything on the redemption mysteries of the crucifixion of Christ, comparable in spiritual interest and power with the brochure of Bishop Nicholson entitled "The Six Miracles of Calvary."

JAMES M. GRAY

This special Billy Graham Evangelistic Association edition is published with permission from the original publisher, Moody Press.

1927, 1928, by
THE MOODY BIBLE INSTITUTE
OF CHICAGO

ISBN: 0-8024-7834-4

2 3 4 5 Printing/LC/Year 88

Printed in the United States of America

Contents

A Note About the Author

Bishop William Rufus Nicholson, D.D., the author and preacher of the great sermons collected in this book, was born January 8, 1822, and died June 7, 1901. He was rector of St. Paul's Church, Philadelphia, December 1874-June 1898, bishop of the Reformed Episcopal Church, February 1876-June 1901, and dean of the Reformed Episcopal Seminary, Philadelphia, October 1886-June 1901. A tablet was erected to his memory in St. Paul's Church on Sunday, April 28, 1907, at the unveiling of which an address was given by Josiah H. Penniman, Ph.D., then Dean of the College of the University of Pennsylvania, and later Provost of the University. From that address the following excerpts are taken, and when Dr. Penniman's permission was asked, he wrote:

> I shall be pleased to have you make such use of the address. It was an honor and a privilege to be invited to deliver it in the first place, and my opinions of Bishop Nicholson

and the great truths that he was continually expounding, have deepened with the intervening years. I regret that men of his kind of faith are so rare even in a pulpit. I have never seen any reason to change or even modify my belief in the teachings of the New Testament, as I received them in my childhood.

Sincerely yours,
(Signed) J. H. PENNIMAN

It remains to add that the sermons were prepared for the press by the Reverend James M. Gray, D.D., and first published in the *Moody Bible Institute Monthly,* of which he was the editor-in-chief.

THE PUBLISHERS

William R. Nicholson, D.D.

by JOSIAH H. PENNIMAN

As a boy, I listened to Bishop Nicholson's preaching, and as a man I knew him as a friend, and through many years I saw him as he lived his life and did his work.

During all that time I was impressed with several traits of character and qualities of mind and soul, which distinguished Bishop Nicholson from other men and gave him in the hearts of all that knew him that sacred place apart into which none other could come.

No one who ever saw him can forget that commanding figure, that gracious and gentle manner, that sweet and kindly smile. No one who ever heard him can forget that powerful influence which was exerted by his majestic presence, as he arose to address his audience, his melodious voice, the charm of the true orator, the learning of the scholar, but infinitely more than all these, the intense earnestness of a life inspired with but a single great thought, the eternal destiny of the soul, and the divine means of its accomplishment. No other thought occupied his mind.

He was supremely a man of one idea. As he spoke and his argument gradually unfolded, it was seen that his manner was not that of emotional appeal, independent of logic, but it was logical to the last degree, and reached the minds and became transformed into action as a result, not merely of his words, but of the reality impressed upon his hearers of the beatific vision of the human soul, redeemed, cleansed, purified, restored to its God, which raised the preacher high above the things of earth and opened to him and to his hearers the very gate of heaven. It was the vision of the mountain top.

It was as a preacher that he was known to most who knew him at all. Impressive as was his preaching, its greatest quality was the complete subordination of the speaker to his message, so that all the power of the trained orator was used to get the meaning of the Word of God into the minds and hearts of his hearers.

Another extraordinary fact about his preaching was that, almost without exception, his sermons were exegetical and expository. Like his Master, he delighted in opening to others the Scriptures, comparing Scripture with

Scripture in a manner that evinced profound and intimate knowledge of the whole Bible and a clear and unmistakable inference that Genesis and Revelation and all the books between them were but one book spiritually, and combined to form the perfect and complete revelation of God to man and the working out of His great purposes from creation to the New Jerusalem. He was a man of one idea, and that idea was The Book, the destiny of the human soul.

* * * *

This leads me to the second great characteristic of which I wish to speak, the simplicity of the man, as shown by the absoluteness of his faith. So great was this faith that it seemed as though, even here on earth, it had ceased to be faith, and had become knowledge. His childlike simplicity of character was shown in his unwillingness to take even the office of Bishop except as it was forced upon him as a sacred duty. His gentleness and humility in that office are spoken of by those over whom he was called to preside.

* * * *

I wish to speak finally, of the learning and

intellectual power by which Bishop Nicholson rose far above other men in his appreciation of the greatness of the Bible and the extraordinary qualities of that book, which is the simplest and yet the profoundest book that has ever been written in the language of man.

He wrought incessantly for the highest education of the ministry. He ever maintained that those who professed to be leaders of thought and teachers of their people should be capable of leading and fit to be teachers. The greatest result of education is not, as some who talk of it in a utilitarian way maintain, the power to *do* things. The highest, the noblest result of education is something subtler than the power to *do*—it is the power to appreciate and understand our intellectual and spiritual inheritance....Bishop Nicholson combined the simplicity of the child with the profundity of the scholar with the breadth of the man who, through books, lives not a life, but the life of the race.

* * * *

He was a great theologian. He delighted in the formulation of dogma as a result of the analysis word by word in the original languages of every passage in the sacred Book.

But he knew that theology is not religion, any more than grammar is poetry. It was religion and not theology, life and not theory, that was the ultimate result of his study. The meaning of every passage was tested by its conformity, not to the teaching of any theologian or scholar or writer, but to the teaching of the whole Bible, and he knew the whole Bible. It was this largeness of view, this taking of the Bible as an inspired whole, that gave to every sermon on every text the power and impressiveness of the whole of God's truth.

1
The Miraculous Darkness

And it was about the sixth hour, and there was darkness over all the earth until the ninth hour. And the sun was darkened.—Luke 23:44-45.

This is the first of the six miracles of Calvary, the chain of signs which wrapped around the death of Jesus Christ and held it fast to the one meaning of eternal redemption. The second miracle was the rending in twain of the veil of the Temple; the third, the earthquake and rending of the rocks; the fourth, the opening of the graves; the fifth, the condition of things existing inside the grave of the just risen Jesus; and the sixth, the coming out of their graves after His resurrection of many bodies of the saints who slept.

Such were the Calvary miracles; all of them in direct connection with the death of Christ. Some of them were from the heavens, some from the earth, and some from under the earth, yet all together they constituted a class of wonders by themselves. Each great sign, in its own meaning and force, marshalled to its place the one line of testimony; and all the six, in solid phalanx, encompass Jesus Christ in His death, defend the truth of our redemption in His blood.

THE SCENE DESCRIBED

Already for three hours Jesus had hung on the cross, and now "it was about the sixth hour"—that is, noon, and *then* there was darkness.

The darkness was "over all the earth"; or, as Matthew states, "over all the land." No one can positively say that the darkness did not extend over the whole of the daylight half of the globe. But if the phenomenon was limited to Judea, it was certainly even then sufficiently remarkable. Indeed, in that case, it had a concentration of force, like that of the three days' darkness in Egypt, while yet there was light in Goshen. At any rate, the darkness did extend over all the land.

But it was not such darkness as sometimes precedes an earthquake, like that at Naples in A.D. 79, when Vesuvius became a volcano. Not such a darkness as that, for this darkness extended far beyond Calvary, the *originating point* of the earthquake which followed it. And this says nothing of the fact that the earthquake itself was not a natural occurrence.

NO! NOT AN ECLIPSE

Over all the land the darkness continued for *three hours!* Therefore it did not result from an eclipse of the sun, for the longest eclipse can last but a few minutes. Besides, it occurred during the festival of the Passover, which always was observed at the time of full moon, when an eclipse of the sun is impossible.

And yet "the sun was darkened," eclipsed, in some strange sense. There was a failure of its light. The darkness was not caused by the absence of the sun—the occasion of our night. It was darkness at noon time, a darkness in the presence of the sun and while the sun was uneclipsed by the intervention of another celestial body, a darkness, we might say, which was the antagonist of light and the overcomer of it. In the ordinary course of nature, darkness being the negation of light, it is light which is the antagonist of darkness and which always banishes it. But the darkness of Calvary smothered the sun at noon! What an impressive thing! What a trembling conception of the almightiness of God!

Did the darkness come on by a process of slow and gradual deepening? In the words of the text, it was darkness at the beginning of the three hours, as it was darkness at the close. All at once from out of the heavens, it shut down upon the scene. It seems to have departed suddenly, and so, we may think, it came suddenly. At the same time, however, as it would seem from the symbolism of the darkness as connected with the sufferings of the cross, the blackness of it grew as the hours wore on. We think this because of the cry of the Sufferer at about the close of these hours. It would appear that the silence of His endurance could be no longer maintained, for more and more intense had grown His sufferings.

How deep was the darkness? We are not expressly told, and yet, there is that in the narrative to show that it was not twilight. It was a frightful darkness.

A BUSY THREE HOURS

Up until the instant of its occurring, what a busy three hours had passed on Golgotha! The Crucified Himself was busy, if we may use the word. What interest He showed in what was taking place about Him! He was audibly interceding for His crucifiers, listening to the cry for mercy of the dying thief, and answering him in that sublime assurance of salvation; recognizing the presence of His mother and the beloved disciple and executing His last will and testament concerning her and him. The soldiers were busy watching and mocking Him, dividing His garments among them, and casting lots for the seamless coat. The chief priests were busy criticizing Pilate's inscription on the cross and venting their indignation. The scoffers were busy—priests, rulers, and multitude passing by, wagging their heads, railing and reviling. All the currents of iniquity surged on unchecked around the cross.

NOW SOMBER SILENCE

But now at this instant of noon, what? Silence, sudden, somber. The very narrative speaks but one word—"darkness," and then is itself silent. The time from twelve o'clock till three is a blank in the narrative, and the reader is made to feel how hushed was the scene.

At the end of that time, when the sun is again shining, all is action again. Jesus Himself speaks, and the multitude moves about. But during those three hours we see only darkness; we hear only silence. The great Sufferer is silent, as if underneath that darkness some huge horror hung over His own soul. And all else is silent. No taunt or insult is flung at Him now. The crowds are transfixed with amazement. The blood is heard dropping. The suspense is frightful. As all hearts drink in the darkness, they are trembling at a certain mysterious fearfulness of the crucifixion.

The gospel historians do not say all this, indeed, they say scarcely anything; yet so illustrative is their suggestiveness that they create for us this whole scene. The little that they say is placed like a parenthesis betwixt the activities antecedent and subsequent—that little is the one word, "darkness." The darkness thus cast its own shadow of silence along the whole three hours, until the thoughtful reader begins to feel how awful this dismal gloom was! And to this implication of their narrative, the historians give both fixedness and fullness by the remark with which they close the story of the crucifixion and its immediate wonders. They tell us that the Roman centurion, having witnessed the things that were done, "feared greatly," and many people "smote their breasts."

CREDIBILITY OF THE RECORD

So far, then, for explanation of the text. But

now may we rely upon it as historically true? Yes, for the inspired historians have written it. We might add to their testimony that of heathen historians who have referred to it, especially the admission of Celsus, the famous opponent of Christianity in the third century; or better yet, the challenge of the Christian Father Tertullian, who, at the close of the second century, boldly says to his heathen adversaries, "At the moment of Christ's death, the light departed from the sun, and the land was darkened at noonday, which wonder is related in your own annals and is preserved in your archives to this day."

But it is enough that the sacred writers have declared it. I, for one, want no corroboration of their testimony. That darkness did come down on the earth and in a simple belief of it, with the vividness of a cultivated Christian imagination, we should place ourselves under its impressiveness, as though we ourselves beheld and felt it.

HOW EXPLAIN THE MYSTERY?

What sort of an event, then, was that darkness? A miracle, a visible suspension of the order of nature. Thus what a visibility of God was that darkness, for none but He, the Great First Cause, can interfere with the regular course of His own established natural causes. It was He, then, who stepped forth from out the universe of natural causes and became displayed to our view as being Himself distinct from the universe—a living, interposing, personal God, standing with "darkness under His feet."

And yet, all the while at and around Calvary there rolled on in all other regards the whole mighty mechanism of natural causes. Creation had within itself no cause which could have produced the darkness. Yet creation itself, with its every law at work, was the scene of the darkness. There was no shock of disturbance to make creation tremble. The Almighty Author of creation Himself put forth His hand and touched His own instrument, striking it in unison with His immediate purpose. But no string of all the vast arrangement was snapped or strained and not a note in all the scale was left discordant.

God meant to bring Himself in contact with our sensibilities by standing out apart from the whole framework of nature, which yet all the while His power was upholding.

When we consider how exclusively the darkness attached itself to the death of Christ, we have the most decisive proof of design on the part of God in so displaying Himself to view. Jesus, the Son of God, was dying. God was appearing. There stood the cross, and there came down the darkness. It was His providential purpose both to authenticate and to interpret the death of His Son.

WHAT IT TEACHES

1. Accordingly, this miracle of darkness *was God's seal to the truth of the Savior's character and mission.*

When Jesus told His disbelievers that He came to save them from their sins, they were offended at Him. When He said, "I am the Son of God," they took up stones to stone Him. "Show us a sign from heaven," they said. Now then the precise formula of their willful rejection of Him came back upon them in terrific confutation. The heavens did give forth a sign, and the very frame of the universe bent in reverential obeisance to the crucified Sufferer on that place of a skull. Even the Roman exclaimed, "Truly this was the Son of God."

2. Secondly, it was especially *the magnifying of the death of Jesus Christ.* On no other principle is it conceivable that God's concernment with His death should have been made so supernaturally manifest and so overwhelmingly impressive.

Now the importance which Jesus claimed

for His death was that of redemption, the redemption of us sinners from our sins. He claimed that importance for it on the night before He suffered, and repeatedly before. Our pardon, our peace, our eternal life, should be secured to us only through Himself, in His blood.

And, if true, was there ever an importance like this? "With what comparison shall we compare it? " The universe, the ages, all earthly interests—is not the whole, in the comparison, as the mere dust in the balance?

WAS JESUS DECEIVED?

Moreover, as Jesus thus claimed, so also did He feel. In His self-consciousness He realized Himself as being made answerable for our iniquities and as bearing our griefs and carrying our sorrows. "I have," He said, "a baptism to be baptised with, and how am I straitened till it be accomplished! " It was the prime inspiration of His life. And although there was in it a joy set before Him, and although He looked forward to being satisfied at seeing the travail of His soul, yet it was also a consuming zeal. It was a drinking up of the beauty of His countenance, a plowing into His face the lines of disfigurement, and the making of Him a Man of sorrows, acquainted with grief.

Did Jesus, then, miscalculate in His estimate of His death? Was His intense interest in it a fanatical self-deception? Let God answer for Him, as, from behind the veil of natural causes, He came down on Calvary with such stupendous effect. God's own sign-manual was that miraculous darkness, and over the cross, the legend, "Behold the Lamb of God, who taketh away the sin of the world."

3. Thirdly, it symbolizes *the inconceivable suffering of Jesus Christ in His death.* God's own miraculous testimony was thus borne to the fact of redemption in the death of Christ. That testimony took the form of darkness, because of the sufferings of that death being inflicted by Himself. It was He who laid upon Jesus the iniquities of us all, and it was He who dropped out of the heavens that thick funeral pall about the cross of Christ. "Smitten of God" was what the darkness attested. The Father's own Son wounded, bruised, chastised, beaten with stripes, by the very Father. It was not merely the suffering of crucifixion; it was anguish immediately from God. The deathsweat of His Gethsemane agony was forced out of Him by the pressure of His Father's hand before the rude touch of the soldiers had profaned His sacred person. The death-darkness of His Calvary agony was the indication of a yet heavier bearing down

upon Him of the same Almighty hand.

NO LONGER ENDURABLE

Accordingly, at about the close of the darkness, but before it had closed, when His ever deepening agony in enduring the Father's wrath against man's sin had become no longer endurable in silence, then in a startling voice, and with an amazement of wretchedness irrepressible, He looked up into the darkened heavens above Him, and cried, "My God, my God, why hast thou forsaken me?"

Yes, God was there in the darkness, and yet, for the time being, in the comfort of His communion He had forsaken His Son. Of that forsaking—His punishment as the Sin-bearer—the darkness, so deep and so dread, was the image and the symbol. Ah! Christ's bearing our sins in His own body was not a make-believe. It was a stern and experienced reality.

HID FROM HUMAN EYE

Again, the darkness wrapped Him all around. Just at His most excruciating sufferings the darkness shut Him off from all witnesses. This, the impenetrable secrecy of those last hours, is that which gives to our imagination the most appreciative idea of what is yet inconceivable. Throughout the previous hours, in whatever suffering He expressed, He was exposed to view. But it was not for human eye to see Him in His superlative anguish. The man's sensibility could not have done justice to that. If His *life* of suffering as the Sin-bearer stamped itself on His very face, as Isaiah seems to say in his fifty-third chapter, and if it caused Him to be recognized as having no beauty that men should desire Him, then those last hours in which His sufferings culminated must have stamped themselves on His person in impressions proportionate to their unapproached severity. Gethsemane is described, but not the latter half of Calvary. Peter, James, and John were admitted into His privacy of suffering in Gethsemane, but God at Calvary drew the drapery of darkness around Him to hide Him from human gaze.

Oh, the mysteries of that suffering! No eye of man might see them. Only at the last may be heard one loud cry of unfathomable woe and uttermost desolation. Yet, in that cry is the accent of assured victory. "Why hast thou forsaken me" has coupled with it the shout of confidence "My God, my God!"

WHAT IT PROVES

So were symbolized by the darkness those

inconceivable sufferings of our Redeemer. And yet, while the darkness was the symbol of the Father's wrath, it was also a proof of the Son's righteousness. None but a person of spotless righteousness, having no sins of his own for which to answer, could be made responsible for sinners. If, therefore, He was the stricken of God, so also He was the Beloved of God. To suffer for man's sin He was indeed appointed. But by that very appointment, as deep as were His sufferings, so deep was the Father's delight in His person and character.

All this shows us what an untold evil and curse is man's sin, since only thus might Infinite Love save us. At the same time it shows us that God's love is so much stronger to save us than our sin is to destroy us.

Great indeed to us is the joy and the glory of Christ's work; but great to Him was the pain of it. At His birth, when the grandeur of results would be especially thought of, the night became light; but at His death, when the process of reaching those results would be the prominent thing, the light became night.

REDEMPTION WROUGHT

When, however, the darkness was gone because of His having passed through it, He was able to say, "It is finished!" Redemption is done! Then after once again crying aloud in trumpet notes of a conqueror with a voice which rent the rocks and opened the graves in prophecy of His own resurrection, He sweetly said, "Father, into thy hands I commend my spirit." In filial trust and satisfaction He, laying Himself down in His Father's arms, so yielded up the ghost.

WHAT IT IMAGES

Finally, the Calvary darkness imaged forth the doom of those who were now crucifying Christ. It was the Father who smote His Son—who therefore would have died had not the Jews crucified Him. But for the same reason that it was competent for God to smite Him for us—namely, that He was a righteous person—it was wicked for them to do it. "They persecuted Him whom God had smitten, and they talked to the grief of God's wounded."

There is a remarkable prophecy in Amos concerning the miseries of the Jewish people. "It shall come to pass in that day, saith the Lord God, that I will cause the sun to go down at noon, and I will darken the earth in the clear day." What an exact description of the scene on Calvary! That prophecy refers to a yet future time of misery for the Jews. The darkness on Calvary was both pledge and earnest of that darkness spoken of by the prophet. In accordance with this, as He was being led to crucifixion, Jesus said, "The days are coming when they shall say to the mountains, Fall on us, and to the hills, Cover us; for if they do these things in a green tree, what shall be done in the dry?" That is, if they do these things to Him, the green tree, the fruit-bearing vine, of whom His people are the branches, what shall become of them, the dry tree? What shall God do to them?

Oh, by the fearfulness of that scene at the crucifixion, all rejectors of Christ shall perish!

Brethren, true believers in Christ, the Calvary darkness is gone, and the true light now shineth. In that light, the path of the believer is itself as the shining light, which shineth more and more to the perfect day. Then our sun shall never go down, and the days of our mourning shall be ended.

2

The Rending of the Veil

And behold, the veil of the temple was rent in twain from the top to the bottom.—Matthew 27:51.

In the previous discourse we considered the midday darkness at the crucifixion, designated as the first of the Calvary miracles. The second of those wonders, the next mentioned after the darkness, is the rending in twain of the veil of the Temple.

It has sometimes been supposed that it was the earthquake which caused the rending of the veil. In that case, we should have to consider the earthquake as the second of the miracles in order. But it seems gratuitous to ascribe to an earthquake the splitting in two of a loose-hanging curtain, while it did not shake to pieces the building in which the curtain hung.

Therefore what saith the Scripture? "Jesus, when he had cried again with a loud voice, yielded up the ghost. And behold, the veil of the temple was rent in twain from the top to the bottom; *and* the earth did quake, and the rocks rent." According to the order here, the rending of the veil was independent of the quaking of the earth. Indeed, whatever there is here of cause and effect would lead us to think that the rending of the veil was the result of the second of the two cries from Calvary, that is, the last, loud, expiring cry of the Crucified. The same cry then would be the cause of the earthquake.

WHAT CAUSED THE EARTHQUAKE?

These two, the rending of the veil and the earthquake, were twin consequences of one and the same antecedent. It was, as we may say, the loud voice of the expiring Savior which split in two the veil of the Temple, and shook the earth, and broke the rocks.

This, the suggestion of Matthew, is strengthened by Mark, who, while mentioning together the incident of the veil and the last cry of the divine Sufferer, does not mention the earthquake. Moreover, while Matthew, in accounting for the impressions of the Roman centurion in witnessing the crucifixion, says that he was affected partly by his seeing the earthquake; Mark, who says nothing of the earthquake, tells us that the centurion was affected partly by his seeing that Jesus *so* cried out.

From this comparison of the two evangelists it is suggested that the force of that cry is to be measured by the quaking of the earth; and if by that, then also by the rending of the veil.

Thus, in seeking for the true adjustment of those two events with reference to each other, we have at the same time discovered a certain relation of cause and effect that is most solemn and sublime. "Jesus *cried with a loud voice*, and, behold, *the veil of the temple was rent in twain from the top to the bottom.*"

And now we should obtain a correct idea of the veil itself.

The Temple succeeded to and took the place of the Tabernacle, but the veil of the Temple was the veil of the Tabernacle perpetuated. There were many differences between the two buildings; but as to the veils, the latter was just a reproduction of the earlier in material and ornamentation, while in regard to their purposes they were precisely identical.

Therefore, although the veil rent was that belonging to the Temple, yet we must go back to the Tabernacle if we would bring out the instruction of our subject.

The veil was a covering of concealment to

hang before the Holy of Holies, or Most Holy Place.

SYMBOLISM OF THE TABERNACLE

There were three divisions of the Tabernacle—the outer Court, the Holy Place, and the Most Holy Place. In the outer Court, the congregation of Israel assembled. Into the Holy Place the priests daily entered to minister according to their office. Into the Most Holy Place no man ever ventured except the high priest, and he only once a year, with blood of atonement and smoke of incense.

In the outer Court, in the sight of the people, stood the brazen altar and the brazen laver—symbols of what is needed in order to draw nigh to God. There can be no approach to Him without passing the place of *bloody sacrifice*, and in that blood being *cleansed* as in a laver. In the Holy Place, in the sight of the priests who had just come from the bloody altar and the cleansing laver, were the table of showbread, the golden candlestick, and the golden altar of incense—symbols of union and fellowship with God. In the Most Holy Place, for the eye of the high priest alone, were the Ark of the Covenant, its golden cover—the mercy seat, the cherubim, and the Shekinah—the cloud of glory, symbols of the throne of God's presence, and power, and grace.

Thus, in the structure of the Tabernacle we have God's own symbolism of such truths as are involved in a sinner's acceptable worship of Him.

THE MEANING OF THE VEILS

Also it was symbolized that there were obstructions to such worship. As long as the Tabernacle dispensation had a standing, the approach to God was very imperfect; for there were *veils* in the Tabernacle. The people in the outer Court were shut off from the Holy Place by means of the first veil; the priests in the Holy Place were shut off from the Most Holy Place by means of the second veil. The office of each veil was the same— that of concealing whatever lay behind it, and of barring a further approach.

By virtue of the brazen altar and the laver, the people in the Court might advance so far; but only those who were priests might pass that veil and go nearer, even to the symbols of fellowship with God; while only the one high priest might pass the second veil and go the nearest, even to what were still more significant symbols of the fellowship of God.

Of this obstructive symbolism in the worship

of God, it is the second veil which was the more expressive; for as the Most Holy Place was the acme of the reality and blessedness of communion with God, so it was with ultimate reference to it that all the ritual of the Tabernacle was conducted, from the coming in at the gates of the Court, up to the high priest's appearance within the oracle.

This second veil—the more expressive symbol of obstructionism, the concealment covering of the glory of God's presence—is the one spoken of in our text.

THE SECOND VEIL DESCRIBED

It was a curiously wrought fabric. Upon the ground-work of "fine-twined linen" were displayed the colors of blue, purple, and scarlet. And those three colors, in that harmony which would result from the intervening of the purple between the other two, were interwoven in one mass of cherubim. It was a screen instinct with the ideas of life and power, and at the same time exhibiting beauty and glory. It hung by hooks of gold from four pillars overlaid with gold. The Scripture calls it a "cunning work"; the cunning of God, for it was copied from "the pattern showed to Moses on the mount."

How impressive it must have been, in the

sevenfold light of the golden candlestick! With what awe it would fill the mind, since it hung there to hide from view the greater glory which was behind it. And by the pictured expression of guardian watchfulness and power in the inwrought cherubim, it was ever saying quietly but solemnly, "Thus far, but no farther." We may imagine the whispered reverence among the priests of the Holy Place.

But now the veil had ceased to exist. It was rent. Suddenly its office was at an end. There it still hung, but the eye might now see *through* it and *beyond* it. As a veil it was gone. All at once, and strangely, too, the concealment had ceased!

It was not as if the house, in which it was doing its office, had been destroyed, nor as if some hand of unauthorized violence had interfered with it, but as if itself had become internally exhausted.

RESIGNING ITS OFFICE

It fell in pieces in its own place before the Holy of Holies, as if resigning its office. No hand of man interfered, and not another thing, from porch to oracle, was either displaced or marred, through all the magnificent building.

It was not because of a natural process of

decay that the threads of the veil parted asunder; for though it fell in pieces, it did not fall in *tatters*. It did not have a rent here and a rent there. It was rent "in twain"—in just two pieces. As another evangelist says, "in the middle"—in two *equal* pieces; thus opening into the very center of what it had served to conceal. It was rent "from the top to the bottom"—in a straight line downwards, and completely through. It was not jerked apart by some intruder from below, but cleanly cut by an invisible hand from above. The statement implies the supernatural and indicates that thus the matter would have been regarded by anyone who might have witnessed it.

But yet more remarkable, the rending of the veil was a grand coincidence. When did it happen? Precisely when Jesus Christ expired on the cross. At the instant! That was the august moment for which the veil of concealment had been waiting; the moment for which through all the ages it had continued to exist in defiance alike of time and of violence. The very instant! As though an inherent intelligence had kept watch within it and now heard the stroke of its heaven-struck doom.

CRY OF VICTORY

Especially, as we have seen, it was rent in

immediate succession to the loud expiring cry of the Crucified. There were two loud cries from the cross. The first just before the darkness had ended; the second after the darkness had passed. The first was an agonizing wail of abandonment; the second a voice of joy. The first was crushed out of Him by that agony insufferable, of which the dread darkness was the sign; the second was the bounding forth of His feelings of achievement and deliverance in the restored light of the Father's communion. The first pronounced the words "My God, my God, why hast thou forsaken me?" The second was a shout, pronouncing nothing, but following the words "It is finished."

His work was done. He had borne our sins. The burden was gone. So then, this second loud voice from the cross was the Conqueror's outcry of victory. As when a weary man, the day's task over, is pleased at thinking of the success his affairs have had and sinks to repose in sweet visions of tomorrow, so it was with an intensely human joy, that ere falling asleep, in the triumph of His purpose accomplished, the suffering Savior sent forth that final shout.

And how real the victory was made evident in the supernatural loudness of a dying man's voice. The Roman centurion was overcome with amazement at it, and the solid earth rocked.

With that shout of victory coincided the rending of the veil. As the Savior finished His work, as the note of triumph rose high and clear from His dying lips, then, just then, as if an artisan's blade had passed swiftly down the veil, all concealment of the Holy of Holies was ended forever. It was a sign of *what* the victory was.

Here, then, is something manifestly divine for us to ponder. It was meant that we should think of it and be taught by it. Not only does the Word of God record it, but the terms in which it is written required that the eye of the observer should be there. It is suggestive of the presence of witnesses, and as a matter of fact, there *were* witnesses. The timeliness of it was one of its most wonderful features. Jesus Christ expired at three o'clock in the afternoon. This was the time of beginning the evening sacrifice, so that the priests were in the Holy Place, in front of the veil, actually engaged in their duties. Yes, God meant it to be seen and meant it to be thought of.

ENEMIES SILENCED BY PROOF

And we may pause here long enough to note how strong a proof of the gospel narratives is this statement of the rending of the veil. The evangelists were bold to publish their accounts in the midst of the Jews and under the very eyes of the priests. Were they ever contradicted? How would it have been caught at and used by those acute and watchful infidels Celsus, Porphyry, and Julian! But no; the enemies of Jesus were silenced. They could not say that never before had they heard of it. The simple statement of the evangelists proves itself. It is the true story of the veil's destruction.

Truly, God meant it for instruction. With what power it might make itself felt may be inferred from the sacredness of the veil, which so controlled the conduct of the priests. Great as had been for fifteen hundred years the sins of the chosen people, violation of the secrecy of that veil had never been one of them. As, therefore, it fell asunder, strange and awful must have been the effect upon the witnesses. And as the sight of it affected the priests, so must their report of it have struck with wonder the excited community. In the great coincidences of the hour, how could it have failed to turn every honest thinker both Christ-ward and cross-ward? What a practical consummation it was of the truth and meaning of the occurrence, when, so soon as the gospel began to be proclaimed, "a great company of the *priests* became obedient to the faith"!

And now to us the gospel record is ever-more saying, "Behold"—look at this great sight—this message of God to the eye—the gospel in symbolism.

Now the way in which the dying Savior's victory was set forth and illustrated in the rending of the veil, we may learn from its consequences to the house of worship where the veil had hung. Whatever the changes it wrought there, such, by analogy, must be the victory of the Crucified.

WHAT THE EVIDENCE PROVES

First, the veil being rent, it became impossible for the high priest to continue to carry *within the veil* the blood of atonement.

Secondly, the unbroken secrecy of the Holy of Holies was now at an end, and all its mysteries opened to view.

Thirdly, the priests who ministered in front of the veil might now safely enter into that typical presence of God most freely.

Fourthly, the people in the outer Court might now advance into the Holy Place of the priests, and thence into the Holiest of all. When the very presence-chamber of God had ceased to be screened off, the spirit and meaning of the first veil also were exhausted.

The rending of the veil, therefore, was the

destruction of the Tabernacle dispensation. It took the meaning out of the entire structure. It disjointed the ritual and decapitated the divine economy of the ages. And since it thus carried with it the demolition of the dispensation, so also it pulled down the middle wall of partition between Jew and Gentile and threw open that presence-chamber of God to all mankind.

Such were the typical results; and now for the real results. How did it come to pass that so obstructive an economy of worship was ever instituted by God? Why did He screen off the chamber of His presence from men and ordain that none should approach Him save under the shelter of sacrifical blood? Sin, sin—that was the obstruction. All the Tabernacle arrangement was God's solemn asseveration that He will not commune with a man whose sin is upon him in its deep and damning curse.

When, therefore, those typical obstructions were swept away, it was signified that sin, the real obstruction, was taken out of the way. What was typically done in the veil was really done in Jesus Christ. This was the victory of His death. He, the sinless, battled for us with our sin, and He overcame it. He, the Sufferer, exhausted in His own person the required suffering for sin.

THE QUESTION OF SIN SETTLED

And so it was that the high priest of the veil was estopped from his office by that shout of triumph from the cross rending the veil. For now the Crucified Himself, the real High Priest, was to carry His own blood, once for all, not into the typical presence, but into the real presence, into the heaven of heavens. There He was to appear, in the power of an endless life, as Himself God's righteousness for sinners through faith in His blood.

Thus has He settled forever, for every one who will draw nigh to God through faith in Him, the entire question of sin and removed every possible obstruction to the intimate fellowship of God.

MAN MAY NOW APPROACH GOD

Now, therefore, the way is opened for man's approach. By faith and in spiritual worship we have "boldness to enter into the holiest by the blood of Jesus, by a new and living way which he hath consecrated for us through the veil, that is to say, his flesh" (Hebrews 10:19-20).

In a word, the rent veil was the rent humanity of the Son of God. In its fine linen we see the righteousness of His human nature. In its suspension by hooks of gold—gold in the Tabernacle being a type of the divine nature—we see the dependence of His humanity upon His deity. In its heavenly blue and its earthly scarlet, and in the gradual shading off of the former into the latter by the intervening purple, we see heaven and earth blending together in His human life in rich and beauteous harmony. And in the mass of cherubim into which it was entirely woven, we see the supernatural functions of His human history.

CHRIST THE PERFECT MAN

Oh, indeed, it was the "cunning work" of God—the humanity of Jesus! Its very excellencies were what made it to be a veil. That display of the Perfect Man on earth was the demonstration of the only kind of man whom God could permit to approach Him. His very excellencies, if that had been all, had been the destruction of our hopes. Incarnation, in other words, had been of no use without the sacrificial death. The veil must be rent.

Most thoroughly His glorious humanity was rent. Rent "from the top," it was God who smote Him; rent "to the bottom," He was exceeding sorrowful even unto death; so rent that now through those excellencies we sinners pass at once to the presence of God. We look by faith into the heaven of heavens. We look with faces unveiled, for, though strong and clear, yet mild and lovely is the glory which thence comes down upon us.

There is neither obscurity, nor reserve, nor the blistering blaze of deserved wrath. "Abba, Father" was never heard from the lips of man till Jesus taught it to us. But now the child finds his way at once to the Father's bosom and puts his arms about the Father's neck.

3

The Miraculous Earthquake

And the earth did quake and the rocks rent.—
Matthew 27:51.

This third of the Calvary miracles has a
significance of its own as a link in a chain of
wonders. Not only was it the cause of what
followed—the opening of the graves—but
also was itself a sign of great range and
power. Equally with the darkness, the rending
of the veil, and the opening of the graves, it
was a supernatural notation by which God
made known the importance of the death of
Jesus Christ and forever fixed the true inter-
pretation of it.

GET THE FACTS CLEAR

In the first place, let us get before us the
statement of fact: "Jesus, when he had cried
again with a loud voice, yielded up the ghost.
And, behold, the veil of the temple was rent

in twain from the top to the bottom; and the earth did quake and the rocks rent."

The shaking of the earth was at the instant of Christ's death and followed the loud voice of victory. His death was His victory, and to the power of that truth the trembling earth gave forth its testimony.

STRENGTH OF THE CONCUSSION

Nor was its testimony of slight force. The strength of the concussion is seen in that *the rocks were rent.* Even if that rending was only a trivial one still it would be evidence of no small violence in the earthquake.

On the contrary, however, the rocks were rent, not in the sense of being merely lined across with just perceptible cracks but in being wrenched asunder into such fissures as to lay open and leave unobstructed the interior of the rocky graves which abounded on Golgotha. It was a trembling of the earth of no trifling magnitude. Accordingly we are told that when the Roman witnesses of the crucifixion saw the earthquake, "they feared greatly."

It was thus a result of the Savior's shout of victory proportioned to the grandeur of its cause, an expressive accompaniment of the death to whose power it witnessed.

EXTENT OF THE CONVULSION

As to how far the earthquake extended, nothing is definitely said. The word "earth" may mean no more than "land," and it may have been limited to the land of Judea. And even of all that land, it was the immediate neighborhood of Calvary which we may suppose would be subjected to the concussion since there was the seat of the disturbing cause. There, beneath the cross, to whose victory it was testifying, the staggering earth would vibrate the most.

PROOF OF THE EVENT

Whether the alleged notices of this earthquake found in certain heathen writers be rightly so applied, we care nothing at all, for within the charmed locality of Calvary, what ancient writer was likely to have been present? Or, whether present or knowing of it only by report, would he be likely to have recognized the Christliness of the charm and thus moved to commemorate it as worthy of preferred mention in the long succession of the earth's convulsions?

It is enough that Matthew has spoken and that he spoke with a challenge to those who were witnesses of the crucifixion. The internal harmony, too, in which this mention of the earthquake holds its place in the history demonstrates it an integral part of the history and pledges to its support whatever evidence there is for the other events in the series of wonders. Neither, to quote another, would it "be right, altogether to reject the testimonies of travelers to the extraordinary rents and fissures in the rocks near the spot." "Of course," he continues, "those who know no other proof of the historical truth of the event will not be likely to take this as one; but to us who are convinced of it, every such trace soberly and honestly ascertained, is full of interest."

THE NATURE OF THE EVENT

So far the statement of fact. Now we may ask, What sort of an event are we to regard the earthquake as having been? We have called it supernatural and referred to it as miraculous. But are not earthquakes of frequent occurrence in nature? Why, then, should we so regard it?

A supernatural event is one brought about by the interference of God. But God's interferences are often put forth in accordance with the established order of nature, as when, in answer to prayer, He causes it to rain. Such an event is supernatural, though not miraculous. There is a specific interference of God in such an occurrence, but at the same time He avails Himself of the forces already at work in nature.

A miraculous event, however, is one which, while being the result of an interference of God, is yet not brought about by His use of nature's established order. It is caused solely and immediately by an act of His will, as when He turned water into wine.

SUPERNATURAL AND MIRACULOUS

Now we say that this earthquake was not only supernatural, but non-natural as well—that is, miraculous. It was supernatural in that it was the result of an interference of God, and non-natural in that it was not the result of any of the natural causes of earthquakes or any combination of them. God's interference was independent of the established order, and solely by an act of His will did the earth reel to and fro.

FOUR COINCIDENCES

In proof of the foregoing consider the great coincidences of the occurrence of the earthquake:

First, it coincided with the death of Jesus Christ. It is so spoken of by the evangelist as to give the idea that it would not have taken place except as accompanying His death.

Secondly, it coincided with the attestations of the miraculous darkness and the miraculous rending of the veil. It was one of a cluster of wonders and is to be considered in the light of the company it kept.

Thirdly, it coincided with the shout of victory from the cross as its own immediate antecedent. It was not the internal fires of the earth but a voice on the earth which caused the earth to tremble; the voice of redemption accomplished—the shout of the Laborer going to His rest.

THE CROSS WAS NOT SHAKEN!

And fourthly, it coincided with the rending of the rocks and the opening of the graves. And strangely, violent as it was, it disturbed no other thing!

It did not displace the Savior's cross, though Calvary itself was shaking. It opened graves and yet not all the graves that were there, but only selected graves—the graves of *saints*.

It seemed as if the earthquake were a living thing, whose divine intelligence discriminated the various dead at Golgotha. It seemed as if it sensed the meaning of that shout of victory and so applied its every reeling movement. It seemed to indicate the program that was to follow and to preintimate the Savior's victory for His saints by His resurrection on the third day. Thus it was a sort of compendium of all the wonders.

Now, because of all these coincidences, how plain it is that the earthquake at Calvary was not such as nature ever causes. Rather it was nature lifted out of the course of nature; lifted solely and independently by an act of God; and so lifted in the specially imposed service of Christ on the cross.

THE TESTIMONY BORNE

And now it remains to inquire what was the earthquake's particular testimony to the death of Jesus Christ?

That is had an attesting function of its own is evident. True, it had a part to perform in the carrying on of the series of miracles; it must open the graves. But that could not have been the sole reason for the earthquake, because the victorious shout from the cross, which was its antecedent, was also the essential antecedent of the opening of the graves. If the earthquake had not a witnessing function of its own, its occurrence was an expenditure of miracles, a waste of work, not at all in the manner of God. The evangelist's narrative produces no such impression. On the contrary, the reader is compelled to think of each of the miracles with reference to its own express coincidence with the death of Christ.

CALVARY ANSWERING SINAI

And how was it with those who saw the earthquake? Did they lose sight of it in the opening of the graves? No, as a matter fact, they knew nothing, at the time, of why the graves were opened and could only have regarded it as a proof of the violence of the concussion. On them, therefore, the earthquake exerted a moral effect of its own. It was a sign in itself.

What, then, was its appropriate testimony?

First, it was Calvary answering back to Sinai. There had been an earthquake on Sinai; there was now an earthquake on Calvary, and the wrath of the former was now hushed in the mercy of the latter.

WHY THE LAWS AT SINAI?

On Sinai God instituted the dispensation of the law. Of course obligation and duty had existed before, but God on Sinai gave His verbal law in recognition of the responsibility and duty thus existing in the nature of things. He did this that He might recall them to the people and build up a defense of sacredness around them.

The law as given at Sinai brought out the exceeding sinfulness of sin. Human sin had existed before, but the utterances from Sinai brought it forth into prominence before men and, stripping it of all disguises, made it appear as it really is—sin exceeding sinful, the blackness of darkness forever.

MEANING OF THE TERRORS

Accordingly, with what visible terrors did He, the awful Guardian of truth and righteousness, invest Himself when He came down on Sinai! "There were thunders and lightnings, and a thick cloud upon the Mount, and the voice of the trumpet, exceeding loud; so that all the people in the camp trembled. And Mount Sinai was altogether a smoke, because Jehovah descended upon it in fire, and the smoke thereof ascended as the smoke of a furnace."

By affecting the sensibilities of men, He would make vivid their understanding; and by terrors of the eye and the ear, project upon men's thoughts the shadow of those more hideous and repellent terrors of the soul and conscience.

Thus was it indicated that so great a burden is sin, so entirely the object of God's overwhelming destruction, that it is impossible for man to rid himself of it. He is helpless and ruined. For, "who can stand before his indignation and who can abide in the fierceness of his anger? His fury is poured out like fire, and the rocks are thrown down by him."

A PROPHESY OF GRACE

It was that men might understand this teaching about sin that such a terrible scene was enacted. Moreover, those Sinaitic terrors were only to be rehearsal; they were not the final infliction of punishment and therefore were meant for the sinner's instruction, and warning, and for kindling within him a longing to be saved. The terrors of Sinai were a prophecy that the great Guardian of truth and righteousness would Himself interpose to do for us what we are helpless to do for ourselves.

In this sense, Sinai was the harbinger of Calvary. And so, "when the fullness of the time was come, God sent forth his Son, made of a woman, made under the law, to redeem them that were under the law." Christ died for us. He bore for us the overwhelming weight of our sins and endured those horrors of which the terrors at the giving of the law were the figure.

CALVARY ABSORBED SINAI

Calvary absorbed into itself the fiery Sinai. By that darkness which drank up the light of day and caused men's hearts to fail them for fear, and by that wail of suffering ringing through the darkened heavens, whose depth of anguish none but He had ever uttered, it became manifest even to the senses of men that this later scene was the more awful and powerful of the two.

THE FINISHED WORK

But, at length, the darkness passed, and the sufferings were ended. Finished was the work of making it possible for God to be just and yet the Justifier of him who believeth on Jesus. The greater terrors of Calvary, in which had been sunk the lesser ones of Sinai, were now themselves lost in the sweet mercies of Calvary. The shout of Calvary's victory was heard instead of the trumpet sound of Sinai's wrath.

Sinai was the prophecy of Calvary; Calvary was the fulfillment of Sinai. Sinai was the sinner's wretchedness and ruin; Calvary, the sinner's recovery and blessedness. Sinai was God's inexorable voice of condemnation; Calvary, God' fatherly voice of pardon and peace.

JOY INSTEAD OF PAIN

Now, therefore, because the quaking of the earth was made to bear testimony to the teaching of Sinai, so also was it made to manifest an equal reality in the teachings of Calvary. As, in the former instance, the earth shook as if convulsed with pain, so, in the latter, the earth shook as if convulsed with joy. It thus set forth that Calvary's mercy is as powerful as Sinai's vengeance. One earthquake was the answer to the other. And meanwhile, from them both together we are taught to say, "Mercy and truth have met together, righteousness and peace have kissed each other."

CREATION'S SHARE IN THE VICTORY

And yet a second attestation was given by the earthquake to Christ's death. It was the impression made by the work of redemption upon the physical creation. Jesus Christ uttered His shout at the achievement of His work, and, lo, *the earth quaked.* That connection was not for nothing. It was creation's expression of its share in the victory achieved. Why should not the earth have been affected by what Christ accomplished on the cross? Did not man's sin bring a curse on the earth? Thorns and briers, inclement seasons, man's sweaty toil, the savagery of brute beasts, and all the countless antagonisms of nature are the footprints of man's sin. If, then, man's redemption is as real as man's sin, should not the earth feel its effects?

Indeed, it would seem as if both man and earth were almost but one vital organism, the whole science of physical geography being but a systematic expression of the sympathy between the two—of their action and reaction upon one another. Is it credible that so great a change in man's estate as that of his redemption could be effected, and creation not have a share in it? And if a share, that it should not give expression to it?

MILLENNIAL GLORY

And when we remember what the Scriptures say of the coming regeneration of the earth—a physical regeneration which shall be the counterpart of the world's moral glory under the reign of Christ—we cannot but see that we have in the earthquake of Calvary not only a pledge, but an earnest, of the fulfillment of those prophesies.

We referred to the earthquake as the earth tremulous with joy. That, of course, is figurative; and yet it is not a mere rhetorical conceit. There is substantial foundation for the figure, and it means something. In Romans, Paul speaks of "the whole creation groaning and travailing in pain together until now," and says, "The earnest expectation of the creation waiteth for the manifestation of the sons of God; because the creation itself also shall be delivered from the bondage of corruption into the glorious liberty of the children of God." He even attributes to creation the feeling of "hope." So, then, we have the authority of Paul for representing the trembling of the earth as a foretaste of its destined millennial blessedness, when "the trees of the field shall clap their hands"—when "the light of the moon shall be as the light of the sun, and the light of the sun shall be sevenfold, as the light of the seven days."

And sunshine, such as earth has never known,
Shall fill these skies with mirth,
and smiles, and beauty,

Erasing each sad wrinkle from their brow,
Which the long curse had deeply graven there.

Yes, in an earthquake of joy, creation anticipated its own regeneration; though still, indeed,

The whole creation groans,
And waits to hear that voice,
That shall restore her comeliness,
That shall make her wastes rejoice.
Come, Lord, and wipe away
The curse, the sin, the stain,
And make this blighted world of ours
Thine own fair world again.
Come, then, Lord Jesus, come.

4

The Miracle of the Opened Graves

And the graves were opened.—Matthew 27:52.

The fourth of the Calvary miracles was the opening of the graves.

That disturbance of a graveyard has a distinct place and importance of its own in the Calvary miracles. Indeed, in certain regards, it is the most remarkable of all we have yet considered, the climax of what has gone before, even as the climax of itself is that which comes after.

In the first place, let us consider the fact as stated:

> Jesus, when he had cried again with a loud voice, yielded up the ghost. And, behold, the veil of the temple was rent in twain from the top to the bottom; and the earth did quake, and the rocks rent; and the graves were opened.

Thus it was by means of the earthquake that the graves were opened. And we may infer that most, if not all of them, were situated at and about Calvary. As remarked formerly, the earthquake would be likely to be most violent at the point of its origin—the seat of the disturbing influence. And that there was a graveyard at Calvary is certain because Joseph's tomb was near in which Jesus Himself was laid.

FIXING THE LOCALITY

Besides, if that event were meant as a testimony to the power of Christ's death, then it is most likely that the graves would be in close local association with the cross. Furthermore, that they were graves close by Jerusalem seems evident from the fact that when the saints arose, they went into the Holy City. It is interesting thus to fix upon the locality.

It is also inferentially clear that the graves were rocky sepulchers—excavations in the rocks, and that their entrances were made secure by doors of stone, for the two statements "the rocks rent" and "the graves were opened" are connected.

DISTINCTION BETWEEN FORCE AND DESIGN

Seeing, however, that the opening of the

graves was thus the same as the rending of the rocks, why set it off as an event by itself?

The reason is that there was a significant distinction in the meaning of the two facts. The rending of rocks was an evidence of *force;* the opening of the graves an evidence of *design*. The rending of rocks gave no prophesy of the future. The opening of the graves was as the budding of the coming glory.

Since the earthquake as an event by itself was not lost in the opening of the graves, as we say in a previous discourse, but had a distinct meaning of its own, so neither was the opening of the graves lost in the earthquake, but had its own identity and value. It is the fourth in this marked series of the Calvary wonders. It was the instant result of the earthquake, as the earthquake was the result of the shout of victory from the cross and thus like the earthquake an answer to that shout. The moment Christ died, the graves opened.

WHOSE GRAVES WERE THEY?

And they were the graves of saints alone— God's children, Christ's people. The mortal remains of no one were uncovered whose soul, then disembodied, had not a saving interest in the death to which the opening of the graves was the wondrous response.

It is a grand conception. Those many graves of God's children, each thus lovingly and individually discriminated, were to His eyes the monumental places of all the world!

And now note that while the graves were opened at the instant of Christ's death, yet the bodies in them did not arise till after His own resurrection—on the third morning afterwards. "Came out of the graves after his resurrection," says the record.

So it is not the risings out of them which is the fact now before us, but simply the opening of them. That opening had a force of its own as distinct from the purpose of it. It is something which was not lost in the contemplated resurrections, any more than it was lost in the earthquake.

Thus it was one grand fact of preparation as must needs be made only at the instant of Christ's death, at precisely the Saviour's own entrance among the dead. It could not be delayed till His return from the dead, although the accomplishment of the purpose of the opening was so delayed.

In all these circumstances, how self-asserting is the miraculous! With an overwhelming conviction, we feel it to have been one of the clearest and mightiest of God's interpositions, one of His most precious testimonies to the victory of the death of Jesus Christ.

In the second place, this feeling of the precious instructiveness seems warranted by the plain requirements of the subject. The fact that the graves were opened at the instant of Christ's death but the resurrections did not take place till the third morning afterwards shows that the opened graves were meant for an *exhibition.*

MEANT FOR AN EXHIBITION

If the rocky doors were opened by the earthquake merely to permit the bodies to come forth, then the earthquake would not have taken place till the moment for their coming forth. But those graves were exposed from Friday afternoon till Sunday morning, exposed before thousands of spectators. No attempt at closing them during the intervening Sabbath would have been permitted to be made. Does it not seem clear, therefore, that the opening of the graves was meant for an exhibition, that it had a testimony to give?

WHAT KIND OF RESURRECTIONS?

Again, why were the graves opened at all? What sort of resurrections were those? Were they instances of what the apostle calls the "better resurrection," the true resurrection body, the body spiritual and incorruptible? Or were they, as in the case of Lazarus, the body merely revived?

Now it can be proved by Scripture that they were the latter, as I shall endeavor to show in a later discourse. The point to be made here, however, is that the opening of the graves implies it, for the idea that grave-doors must be removed for the exit of spiritual bodies is self-contradictory. A spiritual body has spiritual properties. Jesus in His risen body entered, independently of any opened entrance, the room where the apostles were assembled, and His risen body, as we are told, is the model of the true resurrection bodies of His saints.

Is such a resurrection then dependent on an opened grave? No more than the departure of the human spirit from the earth is dependent on the breaking down of the walls and ceiling of the room whence it takes its departure.

CHRIST'S RESURRECTION DIFFERENT

See the demonstration of this in the coming forth of the body of Jesus Christ from the grave. A great stone was rolled to the door of His sepulcher; but when He left the sepulcher, that stone had not yet been rolled away. It was removed soon after, to show the disciples that the sepulcher was empty, thus convincing them of His resurrection. An angel came down from heaven to do it. But at the moment of its being done, Christ was not there.

On the other hand, when Lazarus was raised, he was called back into his former natural body, and hence the command was first given, "Take ye away the stone."

For these reasons the opening of those Calvary graves can be harmonized with this conclusion alone, that the resurrections out of them were only the natural bodies revived and not their final resurrection.

REVIVED NOT RISEN

Those saints were not, in their own persons, an adequate expression of the victory of Christ since, in the sense of the fifteenth chapter of 1 Corinthians, they were not yet risen from the dead but only revived from the dead.

But that revival, in itself so stupendous an event, was nevertheless the illustration and certification of the better resurrection. When Jesus said, "I am the resurrection and the life," He revived the body of Lazarus in figurative illustration of the truth of what He said, while yet it was not the true realization of His saying.

WHY A LIMITED NUMBER?

And now we have it explained why only a limited number of graves were opened. It was not their final resurrection; it was not an essential discrimination between saints themselves. God's saints are all dear to Him, but the reviving of a few of their number was enough for the purpose of the present instruction and at the same time sufficient to do worthy tribute to the occasion.

Graves enough were opened to furnish a specimen of the power of the cross, and whatever of that power was taught by those opened graves was taught to all of God's people for all time.

And now, in the third place, what was that which is here taught?

A symbol is a sign included in the idea it represents. A lamb is the symbol of meekness, because the lamb is unresisting, although the human meekness it symbolizes is of a superior quality. Under the Old Testament a slain lamb was the symbol of Christ crucified, because its shed blood actually expiated certain ceremonial offences; although a ceremonial expiation was as nothing compared with the real expiation of sins by Christ.

SYMBOL OF THE GLORIOUS RESURRECTION

And so the opening of the graves was the symbol of the rending asunder of all obstructions to the glorious resurrection in the body spiritual and incorruptible, because it was the actual rending asunder of such obstructions as were in the way of the coming forth of simply revived bodies. Mere grave-doors, albeit of rock, are but flimsy barriers as compared with the difficulties of the true resurrection of the dead.

Accordingly it was thus signified that the better resurrection was now opened. Whatever had made it impossible for the bodies of the saints sown in corruption to be raised in incorruption, whatever had made such resurrection impossible, was now, by the token of those opened graves, taken out of the way.

And since the resurrection body implies the presence of the spirit to which it belongs, therefore whatever had made it impossible for the disembodied spirits of the saints to leave Hades and become clothed upon with such magnificence of bodily life, that, too, by the token of those opened graves, was now taken out of the way.

Thus, opened Hades was the counterpart of opened graves. That is to say, the whole of death, the spirit's separation from the body as well as the body's corruptibility and dissolution, was now virtually abolished for the saints.

Every sainted spirit in Hades could then have been removed from thence and have been reunited to its body in incorruptibility and glory. There was no obstacle against it, and it had now become only a question of God's appointed time.

SAINTS NOT NOW IN HADES

And in pursuance of the victory so wrought out, into Hades—that is, into the interior of the earth itself, where God's dead were comforted, though not in free blessedness—God's dead go no more. Ever since the resurrection and ascension of Christ they have ascended to Him far above all heavens.

Not only so, but God's dead, who had gone there (into Hades), Jesus brought away with Him when He Himself returned from there, and carried with Him above the heavens. The gates of Hades did not prevail against His church.

How symbolically beautiful, then, that it was by the earthquake the graves were opened! In other words, the victory of the Savior's death had passed through to the sainted souls in "the heart of the earth" and had overthrown the gates of their enclosure!

That victory at the center was felt at the surface, and the trembling earth and rending rocks gave token of the joyous revolution effected for the saints in Hades.

WHAT SAINTS ARE WAITING FOR

We thus see that a part of what was done for the spirit, as symbolized by the opening of the graves, has already become actual in the experience of departed saints.

Meanwhile, that which was done for the body, as in like manner symbolized, all saints are yet waiting for. It was virtually done and is as real as though it had now become actual.

Every obstruction to the full resurrection blessedness of the soul, and to the full resurrection glory of the body, was rent asunder, and we saints only wait for the appointed time of our manifestation.

And now it was the death of Jesus Christ which effected so sublime a victory for us. This is the further lesson of our subject.

When were the graves opened? Precisely at the instant of His death. That instant is made all the more emphatic because the dead bodies were not revived to life till the third morning afterward when Christ Himself arose. The graves were opened, notwithstanding that the actual coming to life was not then to take place. It signified a specific connection between the death of Christ and the opening of the graves.

CHRIST DESTROYED THE POWER OF DEATH

Christ's death opened the graves. That is to say, His death destroyed the power of death. The power of death is sin. Death entered into the world by sin and is the penalty of sin. Therefore, the dying of Jesus Christ, who had no sin of His own, was His bearing for His people the penalty of sin.

But death is mainly the separation of the soul from the life of God, the dissolution of the body being scarcely more than a mere shadow of death.

Therefore, in dying and bearing for His people the penalty of sin, Jesus Christ died not alone as to His body, but also, and more fearfully, in the awful inflictions upon His soul. He was made a curse for us, that we might be redeemed from the curse.

Thus, He exhausted the penalty of sin in our behalf and made it possible to take away from us all the condemnation of sin.

Hence the symbolical fact of the opening of the graves at the instant of His death. The death-power of sin was broken by His death, and all obstructions to our attaining to the true life both of soul and of body were entirely removed.

THE TRUTH OF ATONEMENT

It is the truth of atonement which is here taught us, the fact of satisfaction to the justice of God by means of the sufferings and death of our gracious Substitute.

Unless what was signified by the opening of the graves had really been effected, Christ Himself could not have risen. He came to take away the obstacles to our attaining the true life, and in order thereto He took upon Himself God's curse upon us. Therefore if He did not exhaust the curse, and so make it possible to take away from us the condemnation or sin, the curse would still have been upon Him, and He must still be holden of death.

There had then been no evidencing of accomplishment, no removal of obstacles, no victory at all, if He had not risen.

Impossible, therefore, that the symbolism should have been other than what it was.

Those dead bodies could not have started into life till the victory in our behalf had been pronounced. But the victory, pronounced in the resurrection of Christ, was the trophy of His death.

THE PRISON DOORS OPENED

His death had set wide open the prison doors, called off the guard, and left the way free. His resurrection was the use of that freedom.

His death secured for His people their resurrection blessedness, in that it abolished the hindrances to life. His resurrection was the bestowal of that blessedness upon His people.

His death is our judicial deliverance; His resurrection our actual deliverance.

His death is our sin pardoned; His resurrection the receipted certificate of the pardon.

His death was Hades opened; His resurrection, Hades made empty. His death is the grave torn asunder; His resurrection is the dead bodies of His saints walking forth from their graves in the life incorruptible and eternal!

SALVATION OFFERED TODAY

Of such redeeming power is the death of

Jesus Christ. "The graves were opened." Accordingly there are no longer any obstacles to everyone being personally delivered even now from essential death. "He that believeth on him that sent me," said Jesus, "is passed from death unto life"; and, "He shall never die."

Whosoever trusts in Christ is now made free in his conscience from the condemnation of sin and liveth the child of God, having already passed from death unto life.

Meanwhile, his corruptible body awaits its appointed time, for now all unobstructed is the path of life from the portals of the grave up into the presence of God, where there is fullness of joy and pleasures forevermore.

THE WORK IS FINISHED

At the instant of Christ's death the graves were opened. Remember that. At the instant of His death all our sins were completely answered for. The graves were not merely partly opened; the obstacles not merely partly done away.

There is nothing left for us to achieve in the matter of our pardon and acceptance with God. We can add nothing to the work of Christ. Our salvation from sin is in Him at this moment, and it is perfect. What you and I must do is to receive Him, and enjoy Him. Remember, "he that believeth not shall be damned."

Just as I am, without one plea,
But that Thy blood was shed for me,
And that Thou bidst me come to Thee
O Lamb of God, I come.

5

The Undisturbed
Graveclothes of Jesus

Simon Peter . . . went into the sepulcher, and seeth the linen clothes lie, and the napkin, that was about his head, not lying with the linen clothes, but wrapped together in a place by itself. Then went in also that other disciple . . . and he saw and believed. —John 20:6-8.

The fifth of the Calvary miracles was the marvelous arrangement of things in the grave of the just risen Jesus. The purport of the text is not alone to assert the fact of the resurrection but to exhibit it to the eye in process. And from this point of view it takes rank with those other Calvary wonders, which outwardly attested the value and efficacy of His redeeming death.

WHY MATTHEW'S OMISSION?

It is noticeable that Matthew, whose account of the Calvary signs is otherwise complete, makes no allusion to the circumstances now before us. And the explanation of that omission is interesting. The striking feature of Matthew's account is its consecutiveness. After mentioning the darkness—the sign of the sufferings of the cross—he speaks of the signs of the victory of the cross, taking as his starting point the second of the two loud cries from the cross and limiting his remarks to the effects of that cry of victory. It rent the veil of the Temple, and shook the earth, and opened the graves. And, as explanatory of the opened graves, Matthew states that many bodies of saints which slept arose and came out of the graves after the Lord Himself had risen.

Evidently, in a statement so perfectly consecutive, there is no room between the opening of the graves and the rising out from them of the saints for a description of the state of things in the deserted tomb.

Matthew mentions, indeed, the Lord's resurrection as the forerunner and cause of that of the saints. But it was out of harmony with his arrangement to have inserted an account of the condition of the tomb, because its condition was not brought about by that cry of victory uttered long before.

After mentioning the first four of the

Calvary miracles, Matthew then describes the rising of the saints, the sixth and last wonder, but omits this, the fifth.

AN APPROACH TO A DESCRIPTION
OF THE RESURRECTION

Meanwhile, what Matthew omits John supplies. John, while making no other allusion to the Calvary miracles, puts us in possession of this nearest approach to a description of the Lord's resurrection and enables us to consider it in certain aspects of its occurring.

Very early on Sunday morning, then, Peter and John heard from Mary Magdalene that the body of Jesus, placed in the sepulcher on Friday afternoon, was no longer there. She also announced her conclusion that enemies had taken it away.

Instantly the two apostles hastened and came to the sepulcher—John outrunning Peter and arriving first. And he, "stooping down and looking in, saw the linen clothes lying, yet went not in." But Peter, "following him, went into the sepulcher, and seeth the linen clothes lie, and the napkin that was about his head not lying with the linen clothes, but wrapped together in a place by itself." After which John also went in, "and he saw and believed."

When Peter and John entered the sepulcher, they did not see the body of Jesus; but they did see the grave clothes. And they saw the clothes in a certain order—"the linen clothes *lying,*" and the napkin for the head being "in a place by itself" and "wrapped together."

Now that this is intended to be the description of a wonderful state of things is evident from the fact that it is the pith and force of one whole Scripture narrative. Just to acquaint us with the exact arrangement of the clothes is the sole purpose of nine verses of the gospel history. Certainly, so great an expenditure of narrative upon it must show how important it was.

THE IMPRESSION ON JOHN

Accordingly, see further what an impression it produced on the mind of John. He "saw and *believed.*"

Believed what? The Magdalene's story of the body's not being there? Surely, after he saw it was not there, it was hardly needful to add that he believed it was not there! Besides, what had the arrangement of the clothes to do with his seeing that the body was not there? Yet it was that arrangement which caused him to believe.

Or, is it meant that he believed in Mary's

conclusion that, since the body was not there, therefore the enemies of Jesus had stolen it? No, for that is what the order and arrangement of the clothes forbade. It is inconceivable that if the body had been stolen, an enemy would have spent the time to abstract it from the clothes and so to arrange them. And why the distinction of John from Peter in regard to believing? Not only is nothing said of Peter's believing, but, as we learn from Luke, upon beholding "the linen clothes lying by themselves," Peter merely "wondered in himself at that which was come to pass," whereas John did at once "believe."

JOHN COMPARED WITH PETER

Is it meant that Peter hesitated at receiving the story of the theft, while John was an easy victim of such credulity? Was Peter so much more unlikely to be misled than John? No, there can be but one meaning. John saw that arrangement of the clothes, and he believed that Jesus was risen. So expressive of a divine interposition was that arrangement that he became an instant convert to the truth of the Lord's resurrection; although till then, as is added in the next verse, he knew not the Scripture that Jesus must rise from the dead.

Now such an arrangement of those grave

clothes as was fitted to produce an effect like this must have been a kind of picture of resurrection, and in that light let us proceed to interpret the text.

He saw "the linen clothes lying," that is, not merely remaining on the floor of the sepulcher, but lying there precisely as the body had lain there. There they were in exactly the position the body had occupied. And the napkin was "in a place by itself"—not confused with the body-clothes, but on the very spot where the head had rested.

It was also "wrapped" or rolled "together," that is, the head being removed it had collapsed and was shrunken. It had not been unfolded, and none of the fastenings were loosed, indicating that it had not been taken off the head but that the head had been taken from out of it. There, then, they lay— linen clothes and napkin too—no bandage undone, none of the folds disturbed, no change in position, but only shrunken.

LUKE'S CORROBORATIVE TESTIMONY

This description is what the words fairly give expression to; and it is that which is imperatively required in view of the effect on John. Indeed it is what Luke expresses in his one phrase; for, while he makes no allusion to the napkin, he says that the linen clothes were "lying by themselves."

With reference to what were they "by themselves"? Evidently the body. They were without the body, and yet they were so lying as to suggest the body. The idea is that without a change of position they could have contained the body, and so were lying by themselves.

THE NATURAL BODY DISSOLVED

The natural body had dissolved within its wrappings and become merged in the spiritual body, a transmutation that no fastenings could tie down and of such buoyancy of life that it could not linger amid the associations of death. It vanished from within the graveclothes and moved on its way through the great stone at the door of the sepulcher (which as yet had not been removed).

Springing from the dead seed beneath the ground, disappearing from within the knots and foldings undisturbed, it shot up, through the superincumbent stone, into the glorious flower of resurrection!

Such is the picture of resurrection left behind in the graveclothes of the risen Jesus, though it is not a description of the act of rising itself. It is remarkable that, while the

fact of the Lord's resurrection is everywhere
proclaimed in Scripture, yet the act itself is
never described. We do not read so much as,
"Then he arose and left the tomb," but only,
"He hath risen."

This is an instance of the forbearance of
the imagination of the writers, almost as
wonderful as the event itself—an internal
proof of the truth of the history, demanding
for its explanation the divine inspiration of
the Scriptures.

We are not surprised, then, that having
before him such a rehearsal of the sublime
transaction, the keen perceptions of John
should have made him a believer. It was an
argumentative wonder, a miraculous demonstration.

If the friends of Jesus had taken Him away
they would not have removed the clothes
from His body; if enemies, they would not
have arranged them. Indeed, no human hands
could have abstracted the body from its
clothes without leaving behind marks of disturbance on both bandage and fold.

THE PRESENCE OF GOD

It was God who had been there. Those
silent memorials, those shriveled clothes so
undisturbed as though by force of their

unbroken adjustments still clutching at the vanished body—such a condition of things was as much a testimony to the presence and power of God as are the dry shores of a pond whose waters have floated upward in the invisible mist to form the clouds of heaven. Only in this case, the power of God was miraculously present.

A PERFECT DEMONSTRATION

And how perfect in all its parts was the demonstration.

First, that Jesus had really died and was buried, John personally knew. Now he is reminded of it by seeing the clothes which had lain upon the dead body.

Secondly, that the body was missing from the tomb on the third morning he now had the proof of his own eyes, for he saw the clothes lying by themselves.

And thirdly, that the body had not been removed by human agency he clearly perceived in the miraculous arrangement of the clothes.

All this progress and consecutiveness of demonstration was realized to the eye of John within the brief space of the tomb itself and at the moment of his riveted gaze.

THE HISTORICAL ARGUMENT

And now notice a remarkable tning. The historical argument for the Lord's resurrection conforms perfectly to the argument evolved to the eye of John.

What is the historical argument? First, that Jesus had really died and was buried, the Jews, the Romans, and the disciples were equally satisfied. Secondly, that on the third morning His body was missing from the tomb, all were agreed. Thirdly, that it was not taken away by His disciples was evident to all, in the impossibility of their breaking through and overpowering the Roman guard. These are the three points.

There are other arguments confirmatory, such as the personal appearances of Jesus and the moral power of the truth of His resurrection as displayed in the hearts and lives of Christians. These arguments, however, were, at the time of His resurrection, in the future and could then have had no effect on an unbeliever. But the three points above mentioned were patent even then to every thinker and have always been the fundamental historical argument. They contain in themselves alone a demonstration such as scarcely any fact in history has ever possessed.

GOD'S MODEL OF AN ARGUMENT

Now these three points are identical with those which satisfied the gaze of John. They were, however, presented to him within the sepulcher, whereas they are presented to us without the sepulcher.

And so that sepulcher scene was God's own model of an argument for the Savior's resurrection. And as we see how the points of the argument on the outside of the sepulcher conform to the divine model within the sepulcher, we are impressed with this specific proof of the overruling Providence, and in the united demonstrations we triumph in our living Christ.

But now glance at other teachings of that wondrous scene.

First, that it was a Calvary sign is at once apparent. What other death in all the course of time had ever such a following? Did He say that He came "to give his life a ransom for sinners"? By the token of those graveclothes as expressive of His rising from the dead, the sacrifice of His life became an effective ransom.

Did He say that He "should shed his blood for the remission of sins"? By the token of those graveclothes, His shedding of blood secured the remission of sins.

Did He come to be made a curse for us? By the token of those graveclothes, that curse of desertion, which projected itself in the noon darkness of the heavens, rolled away the curse from all who are His.

Did He come to deliver us from every disability and introduce us into the perfected blessedness of resurrection? By the token of those graveclothes, He became the first instance of completed deliverance from sin and death, and the specimen and forerunner of the risen man.

Thus, for all His own, that Calvary death was the destruction of death; for because His death was indeed efficacious, therefore He arose.

THE NATURAL BODY AND THE SPIRITUAL BODY

Secondly, the body which lay in the grave was the foundation of His resurrection body. The disappearance of that body is here set forth as identical with His resurrection. His body was not there, and straightway John believed He had risen. While the body disappeared, the clothes remained behind, thus identifying His buried body as that which furnished forth His risen body.

Wherefore it is not true, as some speak,

that the resurrection bodies of the saints are eliminated from their mortal bodies at the instant of death. The resurrection of Christ is, as Scripture says, the model of ours. The spiritual and incorruptible body will be furnished forth from the natural and corruptible body but for every saint dead or living, only at a time yet future.

And, since Christ's risen body is the model of what ours are to be then, however the particles of our bodies may be scattered, by the token of those graveclothes, the mysterious identity of our bodies is declared to be imperishable, one and indivisible.

THE NATURE OF THE RESURRECTION BODY

And yet it is not implied that the same particles, numerically considered, must reappear in the risen body any more than the buried seed, by which Paul illustrates the subject, is reproduced in just the same numerical particles in the plant to which it has given rise. Yet the buried seed is the foundation and source of the plant—its own identity passing into the plant, and out of its own ugliness and decay there spring forth the wondrous stalk, the leaf, the flower, and the fruit.

Thirdly, the resurrection body, while yet a

veritable body, is a body not according to the flesh, but according to the spirit. A real material body, but meanwhile according to the spirit. That is, not that it is itself turned into spirit, but so fashioned, refined, and qualified that it is perfectly fitted, in all regards, to be the companion of the human spirit.

JESUS' RESURRECTION COMPARED
WITH THAT OF LAZARUS

This truth is illustrated for us in that vanishing of the body of Jesus from out of those wrappings of the grave! Jesus left behind him the clothing of the sepulcher, but Lazarus came forth "bound hand and foot with graveclothes."

Now mark the corresponding difference. Lazarus returned to the same life as before; Jesus did not. The former came back to a body according to the flesh, with the same infirmities and liabilities as before; the latter did not. The former died again, and even now awaiteth "a better resurrection"; the latter dieth no more. What symbolical relics, then, were those deserted graveclothes in the Lord's sepulcher!

That the Lord had the infirmities of the flesh (though without sin) before He had died and risen, we know; but He never had an infirmity afterwards. He once was a weary traveler, footsore and exhausted. After He was risen, and while conversing with the two disciples at Emmaus, when their eyes were opened to recognize Him, He vanished out of their sight, precisely as He had evaded, without loosing them, the fastenings of the grave.

Hence, a true resurrection is very different from mere revivification. Lazarus, though in one sense risen from the dead, was still a mortal man among fellow mortals.

The true resurrection body, while yet a veritable body, is a body not according to the flesh but according to the spirit. When Jesus Christ left behind Him His graveclothes, it was symbolized that He had got rid of the flesh as flesh, that is of the infirmity and obstructive density, which characterize the flesh as it is born into this world. And when He left behind Him His graveclothes, just emptying them of Himself and vanishing from within them, it was shown that He had attained to a spirituality of bodily condition. This is a condition independent of the laws of gross matter, and having such power of motion as when the wind blows, you cannot tell whence it cometh or whither it goeth. This is a condition of body incorruptible, fleet as light, never weary, grand, glorious.

CHRIST'S GLORY THE BELIEVER'S GLORY

Thus the resurrection of Jesus Christ was the perfection, the consummation, of His incarnation. He then became man as He will forever remain man—not in "likeness of sinful flesh," in which human condition He was but a sojourner, but in a renovated humanity and in the "power of an endless life." Accordingly, the people of Christ are destined to the same condition of body and the same unchangeable glory; for He is the Head, they are the members. Even now their life is hid with Christ in God, and their citizenship is in heaven; from whence also, as saith the apostle, they are looking for the Savior, who shall change their vile body, that it may be fashioned like unto His own glorious body.

O delightful hope, wherein rejoices the believer in Christ!

THE FALSE PRIDE OF MEN

And now, by this blessed hope, how false are the pride and self-sufficings of men! They speak of progress and improvement, of individual and social advancement. From a mortal point of view, it is by no means to be undervalued, yet it is all but a change of location on one and the same level. There is never any getting above the ills and weaknesses of this mortal life, and so there is never any radical, satisfying improvement. Our perfecting is only in Christ. And not till the manifestation of that great city of God, whose gorgeous vision closes the Word of God, will man's dream of perfection ever be realized.

On the jasper threshold standing,
Like a pilgrim safely landing,
See, the strange, bright scene expanding;
   Ah, 'tis heaven at last!
What a city! What a glory!
Far beyond the brightest story
Of the ages old and hoary;
   Ah, 'tis heaven at last!
Christ Himself the living splendor,
Christ the sunlight, mild and tender;
Praises to the Lamb we render;
   Ah, 'tis heaven at last!

6
Revivals to Life in the Calvary Graveyard

And many bodies of the saints which slept, arose, and came out of the graves after his resurrection, and went into the holy city, and appeared unto many.—Matthew 27:52-53.

The sixth of the Calvary miracles was the revivals to life that accompanied the resurrection of Jesus Christ.

The text reveals to us that certain graves were opened by the earthquake at the death of Christ, and that the dead bodies arose and came out of them after Christ Himself had risen, and that they went into Jerusalem and appeared to many. It is a statement of one of the grandest miracles, a gigantic piece of supernaturalism, supernatural in the sense of being wholly miraculous.

Let us review the historical truth of this statement. If it be asked how much may be said for its historical character, it is answered, as much as for the historicalness of all Scripture. By the suffrages of universal scholarship—and in some instances reluctant suffrages—these words are *not* an interpolation, but a part of the genuine words of the Bible. And if there be in all the world a document more absolutely historical than the Bible, it is yet to be discovered.

IS IT AN INVENTION?

But may not the evangelist have drawn on his imagination and out of some such ordinary fact as an exposure of dead bodies in graves have constructed a myth of their rising from the dead? No, if the Bible is the Holy Spirit's words of truth and soberness, it precludes any writer from inventing his facts to gratify a propensity for the marvelous.

"But," as some have said, "it is difficult to account for such a transaction, and the words are extremely obscure." This is not true. The statement that the bodies arose and went into Jerusalem is not obscure. These words are self-luminous and their meaning as visible as light. The difficulty of accounting for the occurrence we are not concerned with, save only to consider it as divinely designed to stand in close connection with the death and the resurrection of our Lord and Savior.

SELF-EVIDENCING MARKS

There are belonging to this statement, however, certain historical marks of its own. Not only is it a part of Scripture, but it is so interlaced with Scripture that it could not but be there. It stands in a line with the miraculous events of the time. It harmonizes with and explains the wonder of the opened graves, just as that wonder was the product of the wondrous earthquake, and the earthquake was the counterpart of the wondrous rending of the veil, which rending of the veil answered back to the shout of victory from the cross whose dying Sufferer had just emerged in triumph out of the almighty horrors of the symbolic darkness! So if that line of Calvary's wonders is historical, then by a harmonic necessity this is the only conceivable conclusion of the great series.

Moreover, it falls in line with the whole teaching of salvation. If we are in sympathy with Jesus and stagger not in unbelief at the mightiness of His salvation, we shall perceive this. Instead of its being incredible that the resurrection of Christ was signalized by such revivals to life in the Calvary graveyard, we would say, upon finding that fact to be of record, "It has the right to be there. It is sublimely credible for it is an expressive pledge of the coming resurrection, when, from all the graveyards of the world, wherever the mortal remains of a saint may lie, this corruptible shall put on incorruption, and this mortal immortality!"

MARVELOUS RETICENCE

Then again, consider the reticence of this statement. In that reticence we see a mark of truthfulness, before which babbling incredulity is forced to be silent and in whose honor the severest criticism must express admiration. The evangelist tells his story of wonder; but we also have a story of wonder to tell of him, which is scarcely second to his own. Our story is that these few words are absolutely the whole of what he says. He tells us that on the occasion of the Lord's resurrection certain of the departed saints arose, and left their graves, and went into Jerusalem, and appeared to many. But he says nothing more. Who they were, how many, whether they went into the houses of the people or only walked the streets, whether they appeared for only once or from time to time during the forty days of the Lord's appearings is not stated. How they were affected by their return to this life; whether they spoke of the realms of the dead or of the recent entrance of Christ into those realms; how and when they finally disappeared or whither they went, on all these topics not a word, not so much as the faintest recognition of the possibility of such questions being asked!

Nor does the writer even tell us whether the risen saints had recently died. At first view, it might be inferred that this is implied in their appearing to many, for why should they appear except to be recognized and identified? And yet Moses and Elijah were recognized by the disciples at the transfiguration although they had never before seen either the one or the other. The Holy Spirit is able to make known to one another those who before were strangers. He is able to do it as easily and quietly as the light shines or as a new thought comes into the mind.

Indeed, the thought in the text is not merely that they "appeared"—which does not fully express the original—but that they were manifestly made known. It is not said that they were made known as to their names. The only thing implied is that they were manifestly made known as persons risen from the dead.

Now of such reticence what shall we say? Did ever a myth in all the range of fiction have so brief a setting? If ever history may be judged by the form she gives her chronicles, then this is history. And a divine history; for what uninspired historian ever practiced a like repression of imagination? Especially unmanageable is the desire to pry into the secrets of the other world. One of the oldest superstitions is that of seeking unto the dead. It was forbidden in the legislation of Moses. It was one of the world's naughty playthings in the untutored earlier centuries. And what a revival of it we witness now in this advanced age, when men think they have attained to the full manhood of understanding!

So, I say, this silence of our text is almost as wonderful as the fact itself. No merely human pen, having said so much, could have said so little.

And now, in the second place, what kind of a rising from the dead were they? Two kinds are exhibited in Scripture. There are six resurrections which were only restorations to this present natural life: the son of the widow of Sarepta (1 Kings 17), the Shunammite's son (2 Kings 4), the resurrection caused by the bones of Elisha (2 Kings 13), the daughter of Jairus (Matthew 9), the son of the widow of Nain (Luke 7), Lazarus (John 11). In all those instances it was only a revival of the natural body which might die again and which, in those instances, did unquestionably die again.

THE RESURRECTION PROPER

On the other hand, there is 1 Corinthians 15, where a resurrection body of an entirely different kind is promised to our hopes in the day of the Lord's coming. "Sown in corruption, it is raised in incorruption; sown in dishonor, it is raised in glory; sown in weakness, it is raised in power; sown a natural body, it is raised a spiritual body." That is the resurrection body proper—the true rising from the dead.

Now in which of these two categories shall we place the resurrections of our text? Were those bodies instances of the resurrection body according to 1 Corinthians 15—spiritual, incorruptible, immortal? Or were they only the natural body revived to this present life, like the bodies of Lazarus and the others to whom we referred? Does the Scripture enable us to answer this question?

Now in that chapter of 1 Corinthians we are told that *all* who are Christ's shall be made alive in the resurrection body there described. Then we read, "But every one in his own order"—every one of the all who are so to be made alive in his own order.

And what is that order? "Christ the first fruits; afterward they that are Christ's at his coming." Christ first—and He did rise in that kind of a body—and afterward, at His coming, every one of the all who are His.

Note it well. The apostle does not say that only such as may not have risen before shall thus rise at Christ's coming. His language is absolute and all-inclusive—"they that are Christ's"—without making any exception. All belonging to Christ shall rise; all who are His out of all the ages. And then he adds, "But every one"—every one of them all—"in his own order," which order he explains as being "only after Christ" and only "at his coming."

Thus how particular he is to tell that in this order he includes all, out of all the ages, who were ever to have part in that kind of resurrection.

Hence, plainly, none of Christ's people have ever had as yet the spiritual immortal body, and none shall ever have it until His coming. Those Calvary saints went forth from their graves, but only in their natural bodies revived. For the true resurrection body they yet wait till the rising together of all of Christ's from all the ages. No one shall antedate another; no one be perfected before another. God has provided some better thing for us, that those saints out of the Calvary graveyard shall not without us be made perfect.

BUT WHAT ABOUT ENOCH AND ELIJAH?

They were "translated that they should not see death," and have they not incorruptible and immortal bodies? The question must be met by the statement of Paul. If Enoch and Elijah at their translation received the body spiritual, then Christ Himself was not the firstfruits, nor is it true that everyone who is Christ's out of all the ages shall so be made alive only at His coming.

It is no objection to this that Elijah was seen in glory when he talked with Jesus on the Mount of Transfiguration, for cannot God irradiate even the natural body with glory? Did not a glory beam from the face of Moses when he came down from Sinai? Did not Stephen's face before his martyrdom impress every beholder with its likeness to an angel? And did not the natural body of the Son of Man become refulgent as the sun? And even when He descended from the transfiguration— His countenance still holding the memory of that radiance—were not all the people, when they beheld Him, greatly amazed?

WILL THEY RETURN?

Therefore, let us abide by the answer of

Paul and be content. Enoch and Elijah may be now in a certain glory, although not the glory of the true resurrection condition. They still live in the natural body; for notwithstanding the corruptibility inherent in it, the age of nearly a thousand years was attained by Methuselah here on earth. Nor need they ever die, any more than the saints who shall be alive on the earth at the Lord's coming and who shall be changed and caught up together with the Lord in the air.

It is indeed possible that God shall hereafter send Enoch and Elijah back to the earth on some service, the fulfillment of which may involve their suffering and death. As regards Elijah, the intimations to that effect are neither few nor faint. But at any rate, as to the true resurrection body, Enoch and Elijah also must wait for us, and they and we shall be together made perfect at the same moment.

Possibly the risen saints of our text were afterwards translated, like Enoch and Elijah, in their natural bodies and did not die again. They may now with Enoch and Elijah be awaiting the future resurrection. Such a supposition may be true or false. We have no authority for affirming the one or the other; but this we say, that they had not, and they have not, the resurrection body of 1 Corinthians 15. And this being the fact, the recognition of it is essential to our instruction in the truth of God.

In the third place, then, what is it that God would here teach us? We answer, truth and certainty of the final resurrection. The teaching is symbolical. The Calvary revivals to life set forth the greater and coming glory. They were not *the* resurrection, but they were *a* resurrection; not the thing itself but the shadow of it. Yet they were a substantial shadow, requiring no less a power than omnipotence. This was the analogue of that, a rehearsal of the more glorious scene yet to be.

Many are the verbal assurances God has given us of that coming glory; but also He would exemplify it beforehand. At the finishing of the work of Jesus and His departure from the world, the great resurrection of the future was fore-enacted in miniature, with an expenditure of power only to what must be put forth for the grand realization of the future—a farewell display of purpose and power which was both a pledge and earnest of the Savior's return to be glorified in His risen saints.

GOD'S PURPOSE IN THE EVENT

What other purposes God may have designed to accomplish by them we do not know; but this purpose surely. When Jesus said, "I am the resurrection and the life," and to prove the truth of it raised Lazarus from the dead, the proof did not lie in the kind of body with which Lazarus came forth. That chapter of Corinthians to which we have referred exemplifies the meaning of Jesus being the resurrection and the life. But the proof lay in the fact that the restoration of Lazarus to natural life, the shadow of the true resurrection, required and actually displayed in like relations the omnipotence requisite for the other.

Indeed, this combination of the historic and symbolic is the feature of the whole series of Calvary attestations. The three hours' darkness, though real, was only a symbol; the rending of the veil, as though an artisan's blade had cut it from top to bottom, was a symbol; the earthquake, which broke the rocks, was a symbol; the opened graves were a symbol; the graveclothes of Jesus, whose marvelous arrangement was a demonstration to John of his Lord's resurrection, were a symbol and here those risings from the dead, living realities, yet only symbolic, were the harmonious completion of the wondrous group.

A GROUND OF ASSURANCE

And now, by means of that scene before us,

how strong and vivid becomes our assurance of the final resurrection! When a thing actually existent has been invested with a representative function, its symbolism is not only a verbal expression of ideas but an acting of them out as well.

It was one of the most beautiful utterances of Jesus when He said, "I am the vine, ye are the branches." Now let a painter put a vine and branches on his canvas, and you have a picture of the vital union of Christ and believers; but only a picture. If, on the other hand, you understand, as you may, that yonder grapevine was planted by God's hand on purpose to stand as a symbol of such a union, you will have before you an analogous work of the omnipotent Creator; and how much more impressive your sense of the union of Christ and believers then becomes!

SYMBOLS AND ANALOGIES

Precisely so, the white robes in the Apocalypse seen as clothing the multitude, while a symbol of the final resurrection and the glory of it, were yet only a picture, for they were not actually existent. But the occurrences in the Calvary graveyard were actual instances of death destroyed for the time and natural life rekindled in the grave—actual instances of omnipotence working in human dissolution and revival. Those revived bodies of saints walking the streets of Jerusalem were designed of God as a similitude, a foreshadowing of the life of immortality and eternal glory; but as actual occurrences, they were also a demonstration of the certainty of that of which they were the similitude.

GRANDEUR OF THE PLAN

Moreover, what an impression is here made upon us of the grandeur of God's plan! In the fact that those saints had *not* the body which "sown in corruption is raised in incorruption" is set forth God's purpose to make the final resurrection a sublime expression of the unity of the Body of Christ, the church.

"They that are Christ's at his coming." No one member of the Body shall have been glorified before another. Its eye, its hand, its foot, its greatest and its least, whether their remains be under the snows of Greenland or the burning soil of Africa, they shall together be ushered into the fullness of eternal life. The whole Body, then at length compacted out of all the ages, shall stand forth at one and the same moment in the finished symmetry of beauty and of glory.

Another lesson is that only in the personal

deliverance of Christ Himself are His people delivered. The saints of Calvary were revived from the dead only subsequently to and because of Christ's own rising from the dead. "Many bodies of the saints which slept rose and came out of the graves after his resurrection."

True, their revival was not their final resurrection, their resuscitated bodies were not fashioned according to His glorious body; but yet they stood in their revived bodies, the sublime symbol of the final resurrection.

Now, as being such a symbol, they are here projected on our view in a sequence to Christ which is both rapid and emphatic. They went forth from their graves, as it were, at the very heels of Jesus. They followed Him, as meaning follows language, as vision follows light.

JESUS FIRST

That is to say, only by Himself exhausting the curse and triumphing out of it in His own person has Jesus Christ succeeded in removing it from His people.

As the Sin-bearer for us, had He not become personally justified before the Father in the efficacy of His sufferings, never could we be justified by faith in Him. And so had

He not attained in His own person to the true resurrection, never could we attain thereto. Thus His people are in Him and are one with Him. His death was their death, His life is their life. *"Because* I live," said He, "ye shall live also."

Oh, the inestimable certainty of our promised heritage! We are bound up with Christ in the same bundle of life. Even now "our life is hid with Christ in God"; and a time is coming when "our vile body shall be fashioned like unto his glorious body."

And take this one lesson more. None but such as are Christ's shall ever attain to the resurrection body of 1 Corinthians 15.

None but "saints" were revived from the dead in the graveyard of Calvary. None but saints, therefore, shall be of that "great multitude which no man can number, standing before the throne and before the Lamb, clothed with white robes and palms in their hands." Those "many" of Calvary symbolized the "innumerable" of heaven.

They who are not Christ's shall rise out of their graves; but it will not be because of the blood that saveth. "They shall come forth," said Jesus, "unto the resurrection of damnation." Instead of its being their rising from the regions of the dead, it will be their plunge into "the second death." Only the saints of

God shall come forth "unto the resurrection of life."

None but saints, and yet *every* saint; for he that believeth on Jesus is a saint, and he that believeth on Him hath everlasting life, and shall never come into condemnation.

Moody Press, a ministry of the Moody Bible Institute, is designed for education, evangelization, and edification. If we may assist you in knowing more about Christ and the Christian life, please write us without obligation: Moody Press, c/o MLM, Chicago, Illinois 60610